SEEDS, STEMS, AND STAMENS

THE WAYS PLANTS FIT INTO THEIR WORLD

BY SUSAN E. GOODMAN

PHOTOGRAPHS BY MICHAEL J. DOOLITTLE

THE MILLBROOK PRESS   BROOKFIELD, CONNECTICUT

To Amy, David, Lisa, and Peter. Thanks for
standing tall in hard times.   S.E.G.

To George and Laura—without them
I might have been a lawyer.   M.J.D.

Photograph on pp. 37, 38 (top) courtesy of Merlin D. Tuttle/Photo
Researchers, Inc.

Library of Congress Cataloging-in-Publication Data
Goodman, Susan E., 1952–
Seeds, stems, and stamens : the ways plants fit into their world / by Susan
Goodman ; photographs by Michael Doolittle.
p. cm.
ISBN 0-7613-1874-7 (lib. bdg.)
1. Plants—Adaptation—Juvenile literature. [1. Adaptation (Biology)
2. Plants—Habitat. 3. Ecology.] I. Doolittle, Michael J., ill. II. Title.
QK912 .G66 2001
581.4—dc21   00-068367

Published by:
The Millbrook Press, Inc.
2 Old New Milford Road
Brookfield, Connecticut 06804
www.millbrookpress.com

CONTENTS

INTRODUCTION

Humans are lucky. We can grab food from the refrigerator and water from the tap. We can put all sorts of things on to protect us from the weather. We not only have legs to carry us around, but we also have bikes and Rollerblades to make moving easier. People have many ways to deal with their changing world.

Plants have most of the same needs we do—but no gizmos and gadgets to help them. Like us, they need food and water. They need to protect themselves. They need to have healthy babies so their type of plant will live on.

Plants also need to fit into their habitat, or environment. If they live north in the Arctic, they must deal with cold. If they grow in the desert, they must be able to handle lots of heat and little water. Seaweed could never survive in the treetops. If planted in the ocean, a tulip would turn to mush.

Plants may not have bicycles or sunscreen, but they do have adaptations that help them fit into their habitat. Adaptations include any part of the plant that helps it live its special life.

Adaptations also include anything the plant does to help it survive.

When we look at this bouquet, the first thing we see is a beautiful group of flowers. But it is also an amazing group of adaptations.

The roses have sharp thorns to keep hungry animals from coming too close. Queen Anne's lace bunches tiny flowers together so bugs can easily find and pollinate them. The freesia's strong smell attracts the butterflies that will pollinate it. Eucalyptus leaves not only turn sunlight into food but they also contain a nasty-tasting chemical to keep hungry bugs away. The sunflower's center is actually hundreds of seeds, waiting to be spread and planted by messy birds and squirrels.

Each plant—whether it is a daisy or an elm tree—has many adaptations. Nature gives it all the tools it needs to fit into its world, find food and water, stay safe, and make babies.

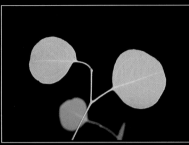

I would like to thank the staff at the Greenbrier Greenhouse in New Haven, Connecticut, and the lovely Leiden Botanical Gardens in Leiden, Holland, for providing access and information on their plants. Helen Bennett of the Arnold Arboretum of Harvard University cheerfully gave advice and a very detailed map of the Arboretum. The plant specialists at the Marie Selby Botanical Gardens in Sarasota, Florida, were able to identify some pictures that I took years ago in Peru. Finally, thanks to Professor Elena Kramer and her colleagues at Harvard University for their identifications and Professor Kramer's technical review of the manuscript.

Michael J. Doolittle

FITTING IN

All living things need water to survive. In some regions, however, water is very scarce.

What's this plant's adaptation?

FITTING IN: DRYNESS

◀ **R**egular leaves lose too much water in the desert, so cactus stems take over the task of getting energy from the sun. These stems also store water. In fact, the pleats on this cereus cactus can unfold to hold extra water. The cereus's vertical shape helps with water loss too. When the sun is overhead and hottest, it only hits the top of a vertical cactus. The rest of the plant is in shade.

In the dry desert, cacti need to trap as much water as possible. The spines on this golden barrel cactus are water catchers. They collect dew into drops that fall onto the ground. The golden barrel's roots spread out just below the surface. They catch the moisture before it sinks through the sand.

▲ **C**acti use their stems to store water. Other plants, like this sedum, keep it in their leaves. The sedum's leaves are waxy so the water can't seep out and evaporate.

FITTING IN

Most plants that live in the ocean must reach toward the water's surface for their regular dose of sunlight.

What's this plant's adaptation

FITTING IN: WATER

◀ **T**he bumps on this rockweed are actually air bladders. These little air pockets act as life preservers lifting the rockweed toward the sun.

▲ **W**ater lily leaves soak up sun on top of a pond. They float because they have big air pockets inside. Their round shape keeps them from tearing when wind blows across the water. Their waxy surface makes water roll off the leaves. That's important because the leaves bring in air that travels through the plant's long stem to feed its roots far below.

◀ **C**oontail looks so delicate; it seems as if a river current would rip it apart. Actually, the opposite is true. Strong currents flow through feathery leaves without a problem. Solid plants are in greater danger of being torn.

FITTING IN

In the cold, soft leaves lose more water to the air (evaporation) than a tree's roots can take in from the frozen soil.

What's this tree's adaptation❓

FITTING IN: COLD

◀ In winter, the oak's leaves create more problems than they're worth. Nature's answer—get rid of them! Every autumn the leaves fall off. A goo dries up like a cork to seal the spot where the leaves were attached so the tree doesn't get infected or lose more water.

During the fall, the oak tree stops growing. Its sap stops flowing. The tree shuts down—hibernating, plant style—until spring.

◀ Evergreens keep their leaves during winter. So these leaves must be tough to survive the bad weather. Rhododendron leaves are waxy so they don't dry out. On very cold days (and dry summer ones), the leaves also curl up. Since less of the leaf is exposed to air, it loses less water.

F ir trees are evergreens too. Their leaves have "antifreeze" sap to ▶ keep them safe in the cold. These leaves are shaped like needles so strong winter winds slip between them without doing damage. A fir's springy branches slant downward so snow can slide off. Otherwise, the snow would pile up until branches snapped under its weight.

FITTING IN

The soil in a rain forest is often very shallow. Yet, some rain forest trees grow very tall. Being tall + shallow roots = a tree that can easily tip over.

What's this tree's adaptation ❓

FITTING IN: FOREST

◀ **I**f you stand with your legs close together, it doesn't take much of a shove to push you off balance. With your legs apart, you have an easier time staying put—even if you get pushed much harder. Buttress roots spread out above ground work the same way your legs do when they're separated. These roots keep many rain forest trees, like this mahogany, from falling over.

With so many trees above them, plants on the forest floor struggle to get enough sunshine. The trillium lives in a forest where many trees lose their leaves in winter. The trillium grows and blooms in early spring before nearby trees get new leaves that block its light.

▶

▲ **T**hey call the jungle a "rain forest" for good reason. It rains a lot. If water lingers on a plant's leaves, however, it prevents them from gathering sunlight. One way plants get rid of water is to have drip tips, the spiky tips on their leaves. Like gargoyles on old buildings, drip tips help drain off water during rainstorms.

GETTING SUN

Almost all plants need sun to live. They use a process called photosynthesis to turn sunlight into food or energy. But sometimes getting enough light can be a problem. Tall plants and trees get it by growing higher than those around them. To do so, they use a lot of energy growing a strong stem or trunk. Other plants have different ways to grab their share of sunshine.

What's this plant's adaptation **?**

GETTING SUN: HITCHING A RIDE

◄ The morning glory spends its energy climbing instead. This vine uses its flexible stem to wind around strong objects and get to the light.

A newly sprouting cheese plant doesn't try ► to find the sun. In fact, it uses the food left in its seed to grow into deep shade. If it can't find a tree trunk nearby, it runs out of food and dies. If it does find one, it starts to climb as shown in the circular picture. Only then will it grow tiny leaves that can produce food. As the cheese plant grows higher, its new leaves change shape and size. By the time the vine reaches the treetops, its leaves are a foot across.

◄ This bromeliad is a different kind of hitchhiker. It is an air plant. It grows high on a tree and uses its roots to anchor itself to the tree's trunk or upper branches.

GETTING SUN

A plant produces lots of leaves so it can soak up the sun. If the leaves shade one another, the plant would be using all that energy for nothing.

What's this plant's adaptation?

GETTING SUN: LEAF PLACEMENT

◄ Many plants arrange their leaves so they can get as much sun as possible. Mint leaves grow in crossed pairs. That way, the leaves cast less shadow upon their neighbors.

Ever seen a spiral staircase? This ginger plant looks like one. Its leaves grow off its stem in a spiral so they don't get in one another's way. ►

◄ If the leaves on this maple tree stayed in their natural position, they would shadow each other. So the leaves shift to find their share of the light. Leaves in the treetops that move to fit together like a jigsaw puzzle are called a leaf mosaic.

GETTING SUN

Trees at the top of a rain forest get plenty of light. Their small leaves have tough skin to protect them from the sun and heat. The plants on the forest floor have a different problem. They have moist air, but it's pretty dark down there.

What's this plant's adaptation **?**

GETTING SUN: SPECIALTY LEAVES

▸**T**his aroid plant traps what little light there is on the forest floor with its big leaves. Each leaf is about 1 foot (0.3 meter) wide and 2 feet (0.6 meter) long—compare them to the dried tree leaves that have fallen upon them. Other aroid plants have even bigger leaves that are 10 feet (3 meters) across.

Begonias live in shady places too. So the leaves of this angel-leaf begonia are designed to use as much of the light as possible. The red pigment on the back of the leaves catches the light that has already passed through. It reflects the light back into the leaves. The leaves get a chance to reuse their leftovers.

▴**S**ometimes too much light can be a problem. The silver linden has a solution. The backs of its leaves are silver. Just like a mirror, this color reflects the light outward. Casting off light keeps the tree from overheating or losing too much water.

GETTING WATER AND NUTRIENTS

People sweat, or perspire. Plants do much the same thing. They transpire, losing water through their leaves. A tree can lose hundreds of gallons of water a day.

With all that water going out, more needs to come in.

What's this plant's adaptation?

GETTING WATER AND NUTRIENTS: ROOTS

◀ **L**ike most plants, this china doll uses its roots to take in water and important minerals. Millions of tiny root hairs absorb these necessities from the soil. They are transferred from the root hairs to the small roots, then the main ones, and finally into the plant's main stem or trunk.

Some philodendrons grow in dirt that has gathered ▶ on a rain-forest tree. A few roots anchor the plant while others start the long journey—sometimes over 100 feet (30.5 meters)—to the forest floor below. When they grow into the soil, they will work like the china doll's roots. Even on their way down, however, they are useful. They collect water from the air.

▼ **B**romeliads have another way to get water. Their leaves wrap around their centers, creating a tank. This tank collects rainwater—enough for the plant and any little creature that calls it home. When other leaves and bugs fall into the tank, they rot, providing important nutrients for the plant.

GETTING WATER AND NUTRIENTS

Most plants get their nutrients from the soil. Some plants have evolved a different way to get their "vitamins."

What's this plant's adaptation ❓

GETTING WATER AND NUTRIENTS: MEAT-EATERS

The leaf tips of a Venus's flytrap look very tempting to an insect. They are an easy place to land. They shine with what looks to be food. Mistake! Less than a second after a bug crawls in, the trap springs shut. The bristles on the leaves point outward to keep the insect from escaping as the trap closes. The plant then uses chemicals to digest its meal. In this picture, one leaf tip has just captured a fly, while a bigger leaf tip on the right is in the middle of digesting another.

The inventor of sticky flypaper might have gotten the idea from a sundew plant. A sundew's leaves are covered with hairs. And these hairs are covered with "sundew glue." The insect that lands on a sundew is there for good. It sticks to the hairs, which fold over and trap it.

The trap on a hanging pitcher plant hangs down from the end of its leaf. Insects are attracted by its bright color and the tasty nectar around its upper rim. When a bug lands on this slippery rim, it slides into a pool of liquid inside the pitcher. Once it drowns, the insect gets digested.

Getting Water and Nutrients

Carnivorous (meat-eating) plants aren't the only ones with unusual diets. Some plants don't bother making their own food at all.

What's this plant's adaptation

GETTING WATER AND NUTRIENTS: PARASITES

◄ The rafflesia is the world's biggest flower. One bloom can weigh 25 pounds(11 kilograms) and measure 3 feet (0.9 meter) across. This huge flower steals its food rather than making it. The rafflesia is a parasite. It uses suckers to attach itself to the roots of a jungle vine. Then it takes the food it needs to live.

The strangler fig ► makes its own food, but it does use other trees to survive. After its seed starts to grow on a host tree, the fig's roots grow down to the ground. More and more roots grow around the host tree and finally fuse together. This "fig column" traps the tree trunk inside and keeps it from growing any bigger. Eventually, the fig tree wins the battle for light, water, and nutrients, killing the host tree.

▲ A lot of people call this plant Indian pipe. It is also called a corpse plant—for good reason. This plant feeds upon dead plants as well as tree roots. There is not one speck of green on an Indian pipe. That's because the plant doesn't rely upon sunshine or photosynthesis for any of its food.

STAYING SAFE

Plants can't run away from hungry insects and animals. They have developed other ways to protect themselves.

What's this tree's adaptation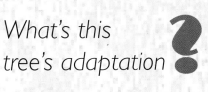

STAYING SAFE: PHYSICAL DEFENSES

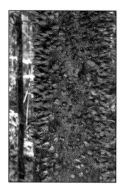

◀ **T**his floss-silk tree has what scientists call bark prickles all over its trunk. No matter what you call them, you wouldn't want to run into these things. And that's the point—a lot of painful ones.

Unlike most plants, grass grows from the bottom of its stem and not the tip. It's a good thing too. Since grass is always getting bent or cut or munched on by animals, that's the only way it can keep growing. ▶

Freeloaders like bromeliads and vines ▶ don't directly harm their host tree, but they can do damage. They soak up water and sun that the tree could have used. If too many of them pile onto a tree, they can break off its branches. This terminalia tree has a great defense. Every so often, it sheds its bark—and with it, most of its unwanted company.

STAYING SAFE

This plant's sharp stingers are only the beginning of its defense. It has an additional way to protect itself against animal enemies.

What's this plant's adaptation?

STAYING SAFE: CHEMICAL DEFENSES

The stinging nettle has physical and chemical defenses. Its stingers have edges so sharp they cut your skin. Even worse, they work like a hypodermic needle, squirting in painful chemicals. Animals that brush up against this plant remember not to do it again.

If you cut the bark of a rubber tree, a liquid called latex oozes out. People use latex to make everything from surgical gloves to pacifiers. Insects that drill into rubber trees aren't as pleased to find this goo. Their faceful of latex soon hardens. If that doesn't kill them, other chemicals in latex will do the job.

It takes a lot of energy to make the chemicals that drive animals away. So this clove plant makes these toxins only when necessary. Tender, new leaves are much more delicious than old ones. New clove leaves contain these poisons and advertise the fact by their red color. As the leaves grow bigger and tougher, the plant stops making the toxins. The poisonless leaves turn green, as seen at the very bottom of this picture.

STAYING SAFE

Spikes and poisons are fine ways to stay safe.
So is teaming up with an ally.

What's this plant's adaptation?

STAYING SAFE: PARTNERSHIPS

This melastoma plant stays safe by teaming up with ants. The melastoma provides sacs on its leaves for the ants to live in. In exchange, the ants protect the plant from hungry insects.

The three-toed sloth is a partner to a special kind of algae. The algae get a safe home in the sloth's hair. In return, the sloth has a coat of living camouflage. During the rainy season when the trees they live in are very green, the algae give the sloth a greenish look. When the trees are dry, the algae turn brown—and so does the sloth.

This may look like dirt on a rock, but it is actually lichen, a complicated partnership between plants and fungi. Algae are the simplest kind of plants. They get food from the sun but don't have roots or stems or leaves. Fungi can't make their own food. They can, however, anchor themselves onto things like rocks. These algae and fungi live together, trading food and security.

MAKING NEW PLANTS

Most new plants are created when male cells (pollen) from one parent combine with female ones (ovules) from another to make seeds. But not all plants create a new generation this way.

What's this plant's adaptation

MAKING NEW PLANTS: VEGETATIVE REPRODUCTION

◄**W**hen a new plant is created from just one parent, it's called vegetative reproduction. In the daffodil's case, a little bulblet grows off the side of its parent. The first plant, or parent, continues to grow. The bulblet can be broken off to make an entirely new plant.

This spider plant ▶ has runners, stems with baby plants on their tips. Eventually the stems bend over or break off. When the babies come in contact with the soil, they grow roots.

▲**P**otatoes are tubers, fat underground stems. We like them mashed or fried, but they are also great raw—food for new potato plants. The potato gives a new plant the fuel to grow quickly. Once it's above ground, the plant uses its new leaves to make food from sunlight.

MAKING NEW PLANTS

Unlike people, plants can't travel around searching for a mate. Some plants rely upon wind or water to spread their pollen. Others get insects and animals to do the job. These plants tempt creatures to visit by offering them nectar to eat. When a bee, for example, zooms in for a meal, it gets dusted with pollen. By visiting the next flower, it becomes a pollen delivery service.

To make this system work, plants must get an animal's attention. Color is one way; pollinators like bright colors they can easily see. But red and blue don't show up well at night.

What's this plant's adaptation

MAKING NEW PLANTS:
ATTRACTING POLLINATORS

◀**B**ats are awake and active at night. White is the color they see best in the dark. Not only is this balsa flower very visible at night, it also has a strong musky smell that helps the bat find it.

Like irises and pansies, this orchid has a road map to guide pollinators to its nectar. The lines on the flower are called nectar guides. They work like the lines on a runway that tell a pilot where to land. When the insect follows the nectar guides, it gets coated with pollen.

▶

◀**B**ees cannot see red. But they do see a color we cannot see called ultraviolet. Ultraviolet mixes with blues and yellows and greens to paint a very different world. To us, the petals of this black-eyed Susan are an even yellow. To bees, the petals are much darker toward the center. This dark center tells them exactly where to go to get nectar—and a pollen bath.

MAKING NEW PLANTS

Restaurants with drive-thru windows often do good business because it's so easy to get their food. Some plants have made getting their food just as simple for their insect and animal pollinators.

What's this plant's aadaptation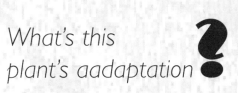

MAKING NEW PLANTS: FLOWER SHAPE

◄**B**ees, like butterflies, must perch on a flower while they have their meal. Snapdragons help bees by giving them a platform to stand on.

▲**F**lowers shaped like a bowl are easy for insects to get into. This mountain laurel has an added trick. Each of its flowers has ten stamens coated with pollen and pinned back in the flower. When a bug enters the flower and triggers one stamen, all of them are released. Each one springs from its holder and whacks the insect with its precious load of pollen.

◄**I**n Thailand, they call this plant the needle flower. Its narrow, tubelike flowers are perfectly shaped for its butterfly pollinators. The butterfly sucks up the nectar through its long proboscis. It's as if the butterfly is inserting a drinking straw into a tall soda glass.

MAKING NEW PLANTS

After flowers are pollinated, they produce seeds. Then they have another problem: How do they get their seeds far enough away so that a baby plant doesn't compete with its parent for sunshine or for nearby water and nutrients?

What's this tree's adaptation ?

MAKING NEW PLANTS:
SEED DISPERSAL

 ◄ **M**aple seeds have "wings" to fly away from their parent tree. When the seed cases fall, they twirl like helicopter blades. This spinning action slows them down. The longer they are in the air, the more time they have to catch the wind and travel someplace new.

▲ **B**urs travel by hitching a ride. They have hooks on their seed case that cling to animal fur and clothing. Eventually, when the burs are rubbed or picked off, they fall to the ground—and a new home.

◄ **A**n oak tree can produce 90,000 acorns a year. Hungry squirrels and birds immediately eat many of them. But they also bury acorns to be eaten later. A buried and forgotten acorn is the same as a planted one.

MAKING NEW PLANTS

Given thousands, even millions of years, plants adapt to all sorts of conditions. Sometimes humans speed up the process.

What's this plant's adaptation

MAKING NEW PLANTS: HUMAN INTERVENTION

◄ **P**erhaps a better question to ask is: What have humans done to this plant? About five thousand years ago, people in Central America decided to stop searching for wild corn and grow it themselves. They used seeds from the healthiest plants for their crop. Picking seeds from the best plants year after year, changed the size, shape, and flavor of their harvest. Today we have many varieties of corn from Indian corn to popcorn to the kind that's great at a summer barbecue.

Taste is only one ► thing bred into fruits and vegetables. Growers know, for example, that most people in this country prefer big bananas with bright yellow skins. So

they have bred big fruit that can travel all the way from Central America to your supermarket and still look fresh.

(EX ◄ **A** normal hinoki cypress tree is 50 to 75 feet (15 to 23 meters) high. This one is less than 3 feet (0.9 meter). It is a bonsai.)\Bonsai are ordinary trees or plants that have been kept small by cutting roots and branches.\ Some people think bonsai is an art, a way to paint with nature. With proper care, a bonsai can outlive its normal-size cousins. This one, for example, was planted in 1787.

PLANTS' REVENGE

Over time, people have bred plants in many ways. We have made them bigger and smaller. We have changed their color, their smell, and their taste. Don't feel too sorry for plants, though. They have affected us in many ways as well.

Take this South American plant, the water hyacinth. Actually many experts would beg you not to take it— at least, not out of its own environment. The water hyacinth has been called the worst aquatic plant in the world.

What's this plant's adaptation?

PLANTS' REVENGE

◄ Unfortunately, when we brought the water hyacinth from South America, we didn't bring along any of its enemies. It has spread from people's water gardens to our lakes and rivers, crowding out plants that normally live there. The problem is growing because the hyacinths are too. Two plants can produce 1,200 babies in just four months.

Plants don't have to be "aliens" to make problems for people. Hundreds of years ago, the Incas built huge cities in what is now the country of Peru. They cleared miles and miles of forest to create their temples and city plazas. After Spanish soldiers conquered the Incan people, the forest conquered ►

their cities by growing back. Archaeologists have cleared part of this Incan city. The rest of it is still hidden from view by the jungle.

◄ It doesn't take hundreds of years for wild plants to take over human projects either. In just a few weeks, weeds took over this tomato patch.

INDEX

ABOUT THE AUTHOR AND PHOTOGRAPHER

Just like plants, people have adapted to fit into their worlds. Of course, author Susan E. Goodman and photographer Michael J. Doolittle have the adaptations other humans do. They walk upright, although Susan limps a little after she's been sitting for a long time. They have eyes that can judge distances—Susan's are green, Michael's are brown. They protect themselves from the environment by living in houses—Susan's is in Boston, Massachusetts, Michael's is in New Haven, Connecticut. And they have both done their best to produce a new generation—Susan has two sons and Michael has two daughters.

As a team, Susan and Michael have traveled all over to create many books, including the Ultimate Field Trip series, *Chopsticks for My Noodle Soup: Eliza's Life in Malaysia*, and the companion book to this one, *Claws, Coats, and Camouflage: The Ways Animals Fit into Their World*. After so much time together, Susan and Michael have adapted to each other quite well. Susan knows Michael will remember how to get somewhere, so she never bothers listening to directions. Michael knows that Susan doesn't always eat her entire dinner. In a restaurant, he orders accordingly.